Lincoln Cathedral's Magna Carta is one of only four remaining original exemplars sealed by the authority of King John in 1215. Hidden in the cathedral archives for many years before coming to light, it spent the years of World War II in America for safe keeping. Churchill is said to have intended the Lincoln Magna Carta as a gift to the American people after the war. Happily for Lincoln, thoug, p fruition and Magna Carta was returned to its rightful home. From 2015 it will reside in its new purpose built home in Lincoln Castle. The story of Lincoln and Magna Carta is perhaps one of the most significant events in English history and is remarkably little known. This book uncovers that story and brings it vividly to life.

Canon Dr Mark Hocknull

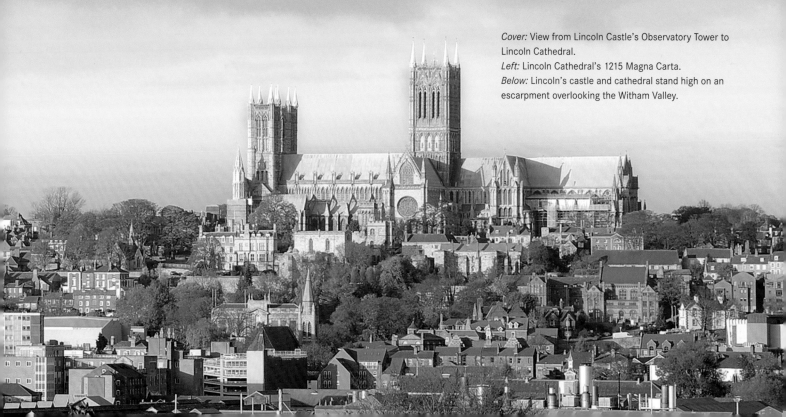

Cover: View from Lincoln Castle's Observatory Tower to Lincoln Cathedral.
Left: Lincoln Cathedral's 1215 Magna Carta.
Below: Lincoln's castle and cathedral stand high on an escarpment overlooking the Witham Valley.

Magna Carta has an iconic status as a cornerstone of civil liberties. It is seen as the source for the ideas that no one shall be tried without evidence, no one imprisoned, exiled, or deprived of their rights or possessions except by the judgement of their peers or by the law of the land. In addition, no one will be denied due process of law, or delayed justice, or arbitrarily taxed. These principles are the foundations of Britain's parliamentary democracy. They entered the constitutions of the United States of America and other former colonies of the British Empire. Echoes of Magna Carta are found worldwide, wherever democracy is upheld. Such basic civil rights are in the daily news, whether it be concerns about the length of time a suspect can be held in police custody without evidence; legislation regarding arrest and detention of suspected terrorists; or debates about limiting the number of jury trials, or eliminating jury trials altogether. Some of these principles were not new in 1215. For example, the Anglo-Saxons had a

form of trial by jury. What is significant about Magna Carta is that it has gone down in history for upholding the rights of the individual against the otherwise limitless power of the king. It places the king under the law, rather than above it. The fame of this document derives ultimately from the four surviving copies of the original Charter of 1215, one of which belongs to Lincoln Cathedral.

A CHALLENGE TO THE KING'S AUTHORITY

King John agreed the terms of a peace treaty with his rebellious barons at Runnymede, near Windsor in Berkshire, in a preparatory document known as the Articles of the Barons. Chancery clerks drafted the terms into the form of a charter dated at Runnymede on 15 June 1215. Copies of the Charter were sent principally to bishops (the royal sheriffs were themselves the target of various of its clauses which they could not realistically be expected to implement). 'Lincolnia' is written twice on the back of the Lincoln Cathedral copy and it is clear that this one was sent to the Bishop of Lincoln. The royal Charter, not yet called Magna Carta, has been in Lincoln since it was first issued, preserved in the cathedral archives by the Bishop of Lincoln, Hugh of Wells, who was present at Runnymede.

Left: Terry Waite, the speaker at the 2010 Magna Carta Lecture in Lincoln Cathedral, was introduced to a former hostage, Lincolnshire's Peter Moore, by the Very Rev. Philip Buckler, Dean of Lincoln.

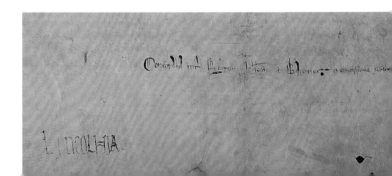

Above: King John, from *A Complete History of England* by various authors (London, 1706).
Below: On the reverse of Magna Carta, 'Lincolnia' is written twice at the bottom in a contemporary hand.

God crowns King David. The ancient tradition of anointing the monarch during British coronations derives from the anointing of Old Testament kings, signifying their dedication to God (MS 30, Lincoln Cathedral Library).

KING JOHN'S CORONATION OATH

At his coronation, King John, like his predecessors going back to his great-grandfather King Henry I, swore an oath to protect his people. This involved both of the duties symbolised on the Great Seal: to defend them against foreign enemies and to protect the weak against the powerful by impartially administering justice.

The anointing of the monarch at his coronation showed that he had been chosen by God to carry out these duties. No one wanted a weak king. Bitter memories of the anarchy of the civil war between Stephen and Matilda were a stark warning of what might ensue without strong leadership. But what were the people to do if the king broke his coronation oath, if he ignored custom and tradition and governed in an arbitrary and tyrannical way? Could resistance and rebellion against a king appointed by God ever be justified? The 1215 Magna Carta was the result of an attempt to resolve this question. At the time no one knew it would come to be regarded as a seminal document upholding civil liberties, still influential today.

LINCOLN'S IMPORTANCE

Lincoln's high status in the time of King John was in part due to John's great-great-grandfather, William the Conqueror. After the Norman Conquest in 1066, William wanted a powerful presence against the northerners in his newly-won kingdom, and he saw the advantage of Lincoln's position. The Romans had endowed 'Lindum Colonia' with a network of roads, as well as the Fosse Dyke, a navigable inland waterway linking the Trent and Witham rivers. The remains of stone walls from a Roman walled city on a steep hill provided an ideal site for a royal castle. Wishing to install bishops in major towns, William ordered his cousin Remigius to move his see from Dorchester, near Oxford, to Lincoln in 1072. There Bishop Remigius was to build a new cathedral, at the northern end of a vast diocese that stretched from the Humber to the Thames. The chronicler Henry of Huntingdon called it 'a strong building in a strong place'. At this time Lincoln was one of the largest towns outside London.

Above left: Matilda's seal describes her as 'Queen of the Romans.' Styled 'Empress' through her marriage to Henry V, Holy Roman Emperor, through her second marriage to Geoffrey Plantagenet she became Countess of Anjou. As Henry I's last surviving legitimate heir, she regarded herself as Queen of England.

Above right: The centre of the west front of Lincoln Cathedral shows surviving Norman fabric.

Below: King William the Conqueror's writ of c. 1072 instructing Bishop Remigius to move the seat of his diocese from Dorchester-on-Thames to Lincoln.

KING STEPHEN CAPTURED AT LINCOLN

The Empress Matilda (daughter of Henry I) disputed her cousin Stephen's right to reign as King of England (1135–54). Stephen disputed Matilda's claim to the throne through the female line. Both took to arms. Around Christmas in 1140, two half-brothers, William of Roumare and Ranulf, Earl of Chester, seized Lincoln Castle, overcoming the king's guards by trickery. Stephen was enraged, rushed to Lincoln and surrounded the castle with his troops. Ranulf escaped and enlisted the aid of Matilda's brother Robert, Earl of Gloucester. On 2 February 1141 the 'First Battle of Lincoln' was fought outside the city. The king's men either fell or fled, but Stephen fought on alone until his sword and axe broke. Robert took the king prisoner, the first time such a thing had happened in England since the days of Edmund of East Anglia, in the 9th century. Stephen was taken to Matilda at Gloucester, then imprisoned in Bristol Castle.

LINCOLN CASTLE HELD BY JOHN'S ALLIES

The castle saw action again, when John plotted against his older brother, King Richard the Lionheart. Richard was seldom in England; he was engaged in warfare with Philip II of France, or on crusade in battles against the Muslims for control of Christian sites in Jerusalem. While Richard was absent on crusade, John plotted with the French king to divide up Richard's lands in northern France. John defied William Longchamp, Bishop of Ely, who was administering the king's affairs in his absence. Gerard de Canville, Sheriff of Lincoln and Constable of Lincoln Castle, supported John. As Gerard was constable of a royal castle, his disloyalty to the king incited Bishop Longchamp to send forces to besiege the castle in 1191, and to deprive Gerard of his office. Gerard assisted John in securing the castles of Nottingham and Tickhill, leaving his wife Nicola in charge of Lincoln Castle. She was the daughter of Richard de la Haye, a former castellan or constable of the castle. According to the medieval chronicler Richard of Devizes, 'Nicola, not thinking about anything womanly, defended the castle manfully.'

Lucy Tower, Lincoln Castle's mid-12th-century polygonal shell keep.

Below: The crowned King Stephen leads his knights up to Lincoln Castle. Henry of Huntingdon, Archdeacon of Lincoln, gave a contemporary account of the battle in *Historia Anglorum* (Arundel MS 48, British Library).

When King Stephen's son and heir Eustace died, the king recognised Matilda's son Henry as his heir. Henry had inherited the titles of Count of Anjou and Duke of Normandy from his father, Geoffrey Plantagenet. Through his marriage to Eleanor of Aquitaine in 1147 Henry acquired Aquitaine, the whole region of south-west France stretching from the Loire to the Pyrenees. On Stephen's death in 1154, Henry II succeeded to the English throne, the first of the Plantagenet kings who were to rule England until 1399. Henry united under his rule a vast empire, stretching from the north of England to the frontier with Spain. England was only a part of his realm. As the power of the Capetian kings of France posed an increasing threat to the integrity of the empire, the Plantagenet kings needed to spend much of their time on the Continent. The focal point of their lands was Normandy and its eastern border with France, not England.

Both Henry and his sons, the future kings Richard I and John, were determined to keep their empire together by strong government. Their need to defend their territories against external attack or internal rebellion led them to demand increasing sums of money from their subjects. They were entitled to annual receipts at the Exchequer from the sheriffs of the counties who collected the rents from royal lands, and other regular payments. These were largely fixed, however, and other sources had to be tapped to meet the increasing financial pressures.

INCREASING ROYAL INCOME

The king had a right to various payments from his chief feudal tenants. When a tenant died, his heir had to pay a relief before he could receive his inheritance, while the right to marry the tenant's widow could be sold. If the heir was a minor, his wardship could likewise be sold. Although the barons wanted these payments to be made at a fixed rate, the king continued to demand as much as he thought the market would bear. The duty of the king's

Above: The seal of King Philip II of France, known as 'Philip Augustus'.
Below: The tomb effigies of King Henry II (background) and his Queen, Eleanor of Aquitaine, at the Abbey of Fontevraud in France.

tenants to provide him with military service in time of war was increasingly commuted into a money payment known as scutage, or 'shield-money'. As the Plantagenet empire came under increasing pressure from the warlike King of France, scutage came to be demanded more frequently, and at a higher rate.

Right: The enamel portrait on the tomb of Geoffrey Plantagenet, Count of Anjou and Duke of Normandy, in Le Mans Cathedral, France.
Below: Map of the Angevin Empire under Henry II.

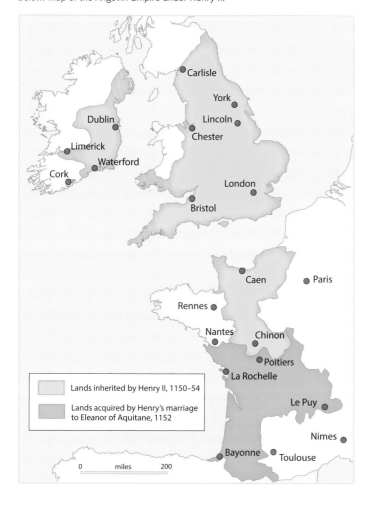

Lands inherited by Henry II, 1150–54

Lands acquired by Henry's marriage to Eleanor of Aquitane, 1152

0   miles   200

King Richard's absence on crusade, and his subsequent captivity at the hands of the German Emperor, gave King Philip II of France an opportunity to attack Normandy, the centre of the Plantagenet empire. Yet such was Richard the Lionheart's military prowess that, after his release in 1194, he was able to recover much of the territory that had been lost. In 1199, while he was campaigning in the Limousin, he was struck by a crossbow bolt and died of his wounds. His brother John, who succeeded to the throne, lacked Richard's qualities of military leadership. In addition, he was cruel and incurably suspicious. He often ill-treated his friends and allies, who turned against him as a result. Even after he was crowned king, John was widely believed to have murdered his nephew Arthur (the son of his elder brother Geoffrey), because he feared a rival claim to his throne.

When Philip II invaded Normandy in 1202, John found himself abandoned by most of his former allies, and the campaign ended in 1204 in ignominious defeat. The whole of the Duchy of Normandy, the ancestral homeland from which John's great-great-grandfather, William, had set out to conquer England, was lost to the French. John sailed back to England with his reputation in tatters. He was not a man to accept defeat, however, and he was determined to regain his lost inheritance. To do so he required money, and he set to work at once to build up his financial resources. He faced a major difficulty because Normandy had been one of the richest parts of his empire, and its wealth was now in the hands of his enemy, the King of France.

TAXES RAISED FOR NORMANDY CAMPAIGN

John had no choice but to exact the money he needed for the recovery of Normandy from the people of England.

The Abbey of St Etienne, founded by William the Conqueror, in Caen, Normandy. When John lost Normandy he broke the link with England forged by his great-great-grandfather.

Ever-higher sums were demanded from the sheriffs at their accounting before the Exchequer each year. The feudal payments for reliefs, marriages and wardships increased sharply. The king sought to squeeze as much money as he could from the administration of justice by the imposition of huge fines. Scutage, formerly reserved for times of military need, became almost an annual payment. Then in 1207 John levied a general tax of a 13th of the value of incomes and moveable property, something that had only been done before in specific emergencies; this raised the unprecedented sum of £60,000, a huge sum, when compared with a labourer's daily wage of 1½ pennies in old money at this time.

This aggressive campaign to raise money inevitably created a climate of fear among John's subjects. Those guilty of even minor offences were said to be 'in the king's mercy' and subject to his arbitrary justice. Those whom the king suspected – and there were many of them – might be required to give hostages, by sending a son or other family member to be kept in custody at the king's court.

Left: King Richard the Lionheart, from Matthew Paris's manuscript, *Historia Anglorum, Chronica Maiora* (Royal MS 14 C VII, British Library).
Above: King John (Royal MS 14 C VII, British Library).

Hugh of Avalon was a monk administrator of the Grande Chartreuse, a Carthusian monastery near Grenoble in the Alps. In 1179 King John's father, Henry II, appointed Hugh as prior of the Charterhouse at Witham in Somerset, one of three monasteries the king founded or re-founded to make amends for his part in the murder of St Thomas Becket, the archbishop who had been slain in 1170 by Henry's knights in Canterbury Cathedral. In 1186 Hugh was elected Bishop of Lincoln, and consecrated in the presence of the king at Westminster Abbey.

Hugh arrived in Lincoln in the year following an earthquake which had devastated Bishop Remigius's cathedral. He set about rebuilding and enlarging it in the new Gothic style. The old west front was retained, but widened and heightened. Behind this front were a wider and longer nave, two transepts, choir, and east end with chapels. It was said that the bishop himself carried a hod holding mortar for the rebuilding. He died in 1200 before the completion of the new cathedral, and was declared a saint in 1220.

HUGH ADMONISHES TWO KINGS

The demands made by Richard I for money or soldiers to fight wars which were not on English soil were rejected by Hugh at a council held in Oxford in 1198. Richard flew into a rage and ordered that Hugh's property be confiscated,

St Hugh's seal shows a bishop wearing a mitre, holding a crozier. His right hand is raised in blessing. The inscription translates as 'Hugh, by the grace of God, Bishop of Lincoln'.

but no one dared to take it. Afterwards Hugh went to Normandy to meet the king. Richard admired his courage and forgave him. Never afraid to speak his mind, Hugh rebuked the king for his infidelity to his wife and for encroaching on the Church's rights.

Soon after John succeeded to the throne, Bishop Hugh accompanied him to the Abbey of Fontevraud, where the bodies of his parents and his brother Richard the Lionheart were interred. Stopping to look at the Last Judgement carved in stone over the west door, Hugh pointed out the presence of some kings among the damned. He said to John:

Fix your mind on their perpetual torment and let your heart dwell on their ceaseless punishment. Thus you will understand the great dangers incurred by those who for a short time are set over others as rulers, but who by not ruling themselves are tormented by devils forever. This fate should always be feared while there is time to avoid it, lest it should be endured for ever when it cannot be escaped.

Hugh knew that John was greedy for power and riches. He wanted to warn him that he must curb his own excesses in order to better carry out his responsibilities as king. Even kings risked eternal damnation in hell if they ignored their duties.

Above: Detail of the north transept rose window, Lincoln Cathedral, showing St Hugh's coffin being carried in procession through Lincoln for burial in the cathedral.

Left: This early 14th-century statue of St Hugh and his pet swan originally stood on the spire of the University Church of St Mary the Virgin in Oxford, which was in the medieval diocese of Lincoln.

To add to John's unpopularity, in 1206 he began a quarrel with the Church over the choice of a new Archbishop of Canterbury. The king's candidate did not find favour with Pope Innocent III, who chose Stephen Langton, an Englishman who had spent many years at the University of Paris, in the capital city of John's principal enemy.

John was furious and refused to allow Langton to enter the country. In 1208 the Pope responded by placing England under an Interdict, meaning that ordinary people could not hear Mass, or take the sacraments of the Church, nor could burials take place in consecrated ground. John was unmoved and retaliated by seizing the Church's revenues. Most of the bishops joined Langton in exile, and in 1209 John was excommunicated by the Pope.

JOHN SUBMITS TO THE POPE

Matters remained at a stalemate until 1213, when the King of France began to make preparations for an invasion of England. As an excommunicate, John could not expect to receive support. So in a dramatic move he submitted to the Pope, agreeing to accept Langton and to recompense the Church for its losses during the Interdict. He also became in effect the Pope's feudal subject, resigning his kingdom to the papal see and receiving it back in return for doing homage and for an annual payment of 1,000 marks, or £666.

John, his war-chest now filled with an astonishing £130,000, was finally able to put his plans into effect for the recapture of Normandy. He made alliances with rulers in Flanders and southern Germany to attack France from the north, while he took a force to Gascony to invade from the south. In July 1214, the attempt ended in catastrophe with the decisive defeat of John's allies at the battle of Bouvines in Flanders. Once again King John returned to England in defeat.

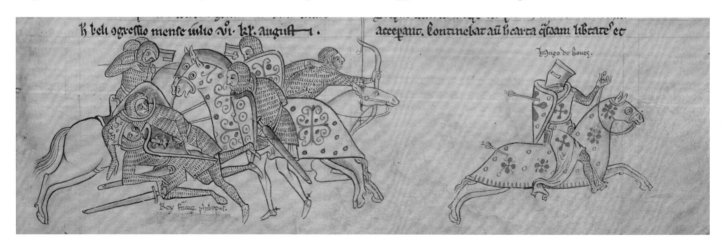

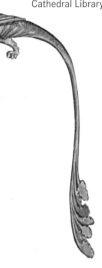

Left: In the first line of Psalm 52, a tyrant wields his sword within a capital 'Q' beginning the phrase 'Quid gloriaris'? 'Why boastest thou thyself, thou tyrant?' (MS 30, Lincoln Cathedral Library).

Right: Pope Innocent III, detail of a 13th-century fresco in the lower church of the Benedictine abbey of Sacro Speco, Subiaco, Italy.
Left: King John's attempt to recapture Normandy failed at the Battle of Bouvines. John's commander flees (right) while the victor, the King of France, is unhorsed (*Chronica Maiora* II MS 16, Parker Library).

LINCOLNSHIRE'S ARCHBISHOP, STEPHEN LANGTON

Stephen Langton was a key figure in the evolution of Magna Carta. Born about 1150, he was one (possibly the eldest) of three sons of Henry Langton of Langton-by-Wragby, a minor landholder in the county. The moated farmhouse west of Langton Church may mark the site of his birthplace.

The young Langton apparently demonstrated aptitude for scholarship. It is very likely that his early education took place in the schools of Lincoln Cathedral, only 12 miles from Langton-by-Wragby and then at the height of its reputation as one of the most influential centres of learning in England. Among the books that he would have found at Lincoln were the commentaries of Peter Lombard, the standard theological text book of the time, based on lectures given at the schools of Paris in the 1150s. Langton himself moved to Paris where he studied and taught.

At Paris, Langton would have known a fellow Englishman, Ralph Niger. Niger's trenchant opinions on kingship, stemming from his outrage at the murder of Archbishop Thomas Becket on the orders of King Henry II, can be found in his commentaries on the Old Testament Books of Kings (now preserved in unique copies in Lincoln Cathedral Library). Returning to England after Henry's death, Niger obtained a prebend at Lincoln where the most significant corpus of his theological writings survives.

Another of Langton's colleagues at the Paris schools was Lothario dei Segni, who in 1198 was elected Pope, taking the name Innocent III. When after 1205 the succession to the archbishopric of Canterbury was in dispute between the monks and King John, Innocent used his papal authority to appoint Langton. The king, outraged at what he saw as interference with his authority over the Church in England, refused to recognise Langton's appointment. The Archbishop remained in exile in France until 1213. Meanwhile in 1208 the Pope placed England under an Interdict.

John's submission to the Pope in 1213 and the subsequent lifting of the Interdict enabled Langton to return to England where he played a significant part in the events leading up to the issue of Magna Carta. His influence on the framing of Magna Carta has been a matter for debate among historians. He may have come to see the Charter as tainted by the fact that it was forced on the king by the coercion of civil war. Rebellion against a lawful ruler (and John was now reconciled to the Church) went against the teaching of the Bible. However much Langton might sympathise with the rebels, he was unable to support them openly.

A statue of Stephen Langton, Archbishop of Canterbury, on the exterior of Canterbury Cathedral.

LANGTON THE MEDIATOR

Langton did, however, play a significant role in the negotiations, acting as an intermediary between king and barons. He also ensured the inclusion in Magna Carta of clause 1, guaranteeing the freedom of the Church. This clause, significantly, was granted 'to God' rather than (as with the remainder of the Charter) 'to all free men'. It refers to the king's grant, 'before the quarrel between us and our barons began', of freedom of elections, making it quite clear that this clause was free from any taint of intimidation. Langton's intention here may have been to protect the liberties of the Church in clause 1, while subtly dissociating himself and his fellow bishops from Magna Carta's later clauses won by coercion and the threat of civil war.

When the settlement between king and barons broke down, Langton's position became untenable. The Pope suspended him from office for refusing to excommunicate the rebels and he went abroad to Rome to seek restoration. He did not return to England until May 1218 but thereafter played an important part during the minority of the young King Henry III. In particular, it was Langton's promotion of Magna Carta as a bulwark of good government that led to its definitive re-issue in 1225. One of the greatest figures in the firmament of European theologians, Langton played a central part in the crisis of government of early 13th-century England.

Above: Detail from a manuscript by Ralph Niger (*c.*1140–*c.*1199), from a collection of six manuscripts held in Lincoln Cathedral Library since the late 12th century. This book contrasts the Biblical kings of Israel with the 12th-century kings of England (MS 25, Lincoln Cathedral Library).
Below: Archbishop Stephen Langton placing the crown on Henry III's head at his second coronation in Westminster Abbey in 1220 (MS 16, Parker Library).

PEACE OVERTURES

During 1213, the year before his calamitous defeat at Bouvines, in the face of mounting opposition from the barons and the clergy, John agreed to accept Stephen Langton as Archbishop of Canterbury, and arranged peace with the Pope. In July the newly-returned archbishop absolved the king from excommunication at Winchester. According to the monk and chronicler Roger of Wendover, John reaffirmed his coronation oath and promised to uphold the laws of Edward the Confessor. By promising to serve the Pope as his vassal, John began to win back the churchmen who had opposed him over the Interdict.

Roger of Wendover states in his *Flores Historiarum* (*Flowers of History*) that in the summer of 1213 there was an important meeting at St Albans Abbey, at which Archbishop Langton and various barons met with the king's ministers. The king's representatives promised reform, stating that the laws of Henry I would be upheld. Another council was held at St Paul's Cathedral in London on 25 August, at which the Archbishop is said to have proposed that it should be demanded of the king that he confirm the charter of liberties granted by Henry I at his coronation. Wendover also writes that the barons went to Bury St Edmunds, Suffolk, in the autumn of 1214 and swore to make war on King John if he did not confirm Henry I's coronation charter. Those present swore they would fight to the death to stand up for their rights.

St Alban's Cathedral, from *Monasticon Anglicanum*, by Roger Dodsworth and Sir William Dugdale (London, 1655–73).

The choir of the medieval St Paul's Cathedral in London, from William Dugdale's *The History of St Paul's Cathedral in London* (London, 1658).

Image of Henry I, from Holinshed's *Chronicles* (London, 1577).

HENRY I'S CORONATION OATH

In 1100, Henry I had sworn an oath at his coronation upholding certain liberties: that the Church would be free, thereby ending the practice of the king collecting the revenues of churches between the death of one bishop or abbot and the election of another; that he would interfere less in the barons' marriages and inheritances, and allow widows the lands set aside for them by their husbands; that he would not force widows to remarry without their consent; that he would be moderate in taxation, and that he would limit the expansion of the royal forests. Henry II and John had issued similar coronation oaths, but there was no way of holding the king to account, and each king could, and did, choose to ignore such promises. But these issues were not forgotten, and they appear again in the Articles of the Barons formulated at Runnymede, and in the resulting Magna Carta.

The collapse of John's plans to recapture Normandy in 1214 left him exposed to opposition in England from those who had suffered from his oppressive rule. The rebellious barons, who were particularly strong in northern and eastern England, greatly outnumbered the minority who remained loyal to the king. John began to fortify royal castles and to hire foreign troops.

At Easter 1215, the northern barons met at Stamford in Lincolnshire and agreed to meet the king at Northampton on 26 April. John failed to attend the proposed meeting, and on 5 May at Brackley, some of the barons formally renounced their allegiance to the king, thus embarking on open rebellion.

In a dramatic move, on 17 May a group of Londoners took possession of the Tower of London. John must have known from that moment that he would have to negotiate. In early June, by 10 June at the latest, the king met with the rebellious barons and prominent churchmen in a meadow named Runnymede, by the River Thames near Windsor Castle.

MAGNA CARTA – A PEACE TREATY

The primary purpose of Magna Carta was to secure a truce in a civil war. The first step was the setting down of a list of grievances against the king, amounting to 49 points. The Articles of the Barons, in which these clauses were written, were sealed with the Great Seal of King John. They begin with the words, 'These are the articles (capitula) that the barons seek and the king concedes.' It was then up to the clerks of the king's administrative office to convert these terms into a charter. A number of copies of the Charter were written and sent throughout England. This process may have lasted well into July. The date of 15 June 1215 written on each copy of Magna Carta probably applies to the date on which the king gave his assent to the Charter. Both the Articles of the Barons and each exemplar of Magna Carta had royal seals attached to them, as a mark of the king's approval and the authenticity of the documents.

It is difficult to imagine that in the heat of the moment the barons could have come up with such a clear plan. It is likely that an undated document in the French national archives called the 'Unknown Charter' was written as a preamble to the Articles of the Barons, perhaps as early as 1213. Written on it is Henry I's coronation charter. Added to this is a series of clauses beginning with the statement, 'King John concedes that he will arrest no man without

View of Stamford from Francis Peck's *The Survey and Antiquity of the Towne of Stamford* (London, 1727).

judgement nor accept any payment for justice, nor commit any unjust act.' This is close to the wording of clauses 39 and 40 of Magna Carta. It specifically promises not to condemn any free man without due process of the law – a key feature of Magna Carta.

Archbishop Stephen Langton has often been suggested as the 'chief architect' of Magna Carta. He is the first person named after the king in the opening phrases of the document, in a list which includes 11 churchmen and 16 barons, all described as the king's 'faithful subjects'.

Right: When the Tower of London was captured by rebellious Londoners, King John realised he had lost control of his capital city.

Left: The Articles of the Barons consist of 49 articles. This document formed the basis of the longer Magna Carta, which contains 63 clauses.

THE ARTICLES OF THE BARONS

Stephen Langton is believed to have taken the Articles of the Barons away with him for safe keeping in Lambeth Palace after the meeting at Runnymede ended. The fact that Langton still had access to rebel-held Lambeth is itself an indication of his ability to pass between both royal and rebel camps. The document remained at Lambeth Palace until Archbishop Laud was impeached during the reign of Charles I. By the 1680s the document was held by Bishop Burnett of Salisbury, who believed it to be Magna Carta itself. The Articles of the Barons are now in the British Library.

Only four of the original charters survive: one belonging to Lincoln Cathedral, one at Salisbury Cathedral, and two in the British Library. Each is on a single piece of parchment, varying in size from roughly 17 to 20 inches long (43cm to 51cm) and between 13 and 17 inches wide (33cm to 43cm). The texts differ slightly in spelling and word order, evidence that they were written in haste by different clerks.

Along with 'Lincolnia' written twice on the back in a contemporary hand, there are two Latin endorsements in late 13th-century hands. One annotation states, 'agreement between King John and the barons', to which another scribe has added, 'by grant of liberties of the Church and of the kingdom of England'. The style of handwriting of the text and the note of its destination written in Chancery script – and the fact that it has been in Lincoln since 1215 – all add up to Lincoln's being the best documented of the surviving exemplars.

The name 'Magna Carta' was not used until after 1217, when the Charter of the Forest was first issued. This smaller document was known as the Little Charter to differentiate it from the bigger Charter. The word 'magna' means big or great in Latin. Magna Carta is often called in English 'the Great Charter' – a title which enhances its significance.

A CHARTER TO RIGHT WRONGS

Some of Magna Carta's 63 clauses dealt with short-term disputes – the removal of foreign officials from the government, the restitution of hostages and of lands unlawfully seized. The majority of its provisions concerned the abuses of feudal payments and taxation from which the barons'

THE GREAT SEAL

For the majority who could not read, the Great Seal attached to Magna Carta signalled that this was the authentic word of the king. The Lincoln copy has lost its seal, but there are three small neat holes at the bottom of the parchment, which show where coloured threads once attached the seal to the document.

The seal, a disc of green wax about four inches across, shows on the front the king crowned and seated on a throne, holding a sword, the dispenser of justice to his people. On the back he is wearing armour and is seated on horseback, the defender of his country. Seals were often detached from documents. Of the four surviving 1215 exemplars, only one retains something of its seal. One of the charters in the British Library was damaged by fire, causing the seal to melt into a lump of wax.

The seal of King John, seated on his throne (obverse) and on horseback as a warrior (reverse).

The barons talk to King John, from Holinshed's *Chronicles* (London, 1577).

discontents had arisen, regulating and limiting payments for reliefs, wardships and scutage, and defining the rights of landowners' widows and under-age heirs over their land. The self-government and chartered privileges of the greater English towns were an issue, especially for the merchants of London, whose trade had been affected by the king's wars. Clause 13 states that the city of London and all other cities, boroughs, towns and ports shall enjoy all their ancient liberties and free customs, both by land and water.

Detail of the Lincoln 1215 Magna Carta.

A CHARTER TO CURB THE KING'S TYRANNY

More general clauses stemmed from the way in which John had sought to impose his arbitrary will on his subjects. Clause 39 states that 'no free man shall be seized or imprisoned, or stripped of his rights or possessions, or outlawed or exiled, or deprived of his standing in any other way … except by the lawful judgement of his equals or by the law of the land'. Clause 40 says 'To no one will we sell, to no one deny or delay right or justice'. Clause 38 states that 'no official shall place a man on trial upon his own unsupported statement, without producing credible witnesses to the truth of it'. These clauses have the most resonance for justice and civil rights today.

At the time, however, the most controversial clause of the Charter was undoubtedly clause 61. This sought to strengthen the provisions of the agreement by establishing a committee of 25 barons who were to monitor the way in which these provisions were observed and, if necessary, to seek redress from the king, with the ultimate sanction of seizing royal lands, castles and other possessions until the clauses of the Charter were properly observed. William of Huntingfield held land at Frampton in Lincolnshire where he had a castle. After he joined the rebels (and was included among the Twenty Five), his lands were seized by order of King John who subsequently granted the custody of Frampton Castle to Nicola de la Haye. After the Civil War she was accused of having seized Huntingfield property worth more than £270.

Born in Wells in Somerset, Hugh of Wells had served two successive bishops of Bath before entering the household of King John. He became an important official in the royal administration, serving the king in England and abroad, from 1199 to 1209. One of the tasks the king gave him was custody of the vacant bishopric of Lincoln between 1200 (on the death of the saintly Bishop Hugh) until 1203, when William of Blois was elected bishop.

Hugh of Wells was King John's candidate to be bishop of Lincoln on the death of William of Blois in 1206. Owing to the constraints of the Interdict, Hugh went to France to

be consecrated bishop by Archbishop Stephen Langton in 1209. This association with Langton angered the king, and Hugh stayed abroad in exile for the remaining years of the Interdict. By the time the bishop witnessed John's agreement to the terms of Magna Carta at Runnymede, John had made peace with the Pope. Clergy like Hugh of Wells who opposed John over his argument with the Pope were by this time reconciled to the king, as John was now the Pope's liege man, or loyal supporter.

Reforms in office systems and record keeping were taking place in the Chancery at this time, and when he became bishop of Lincoln, Hugh II put his experience to good use. He was the first bishop in England to introduce episcopal registration. This meant the recording of the bishop's visits to monasteries and other religious houses, visits to parishes, confirmations, ordinations, and correspondence. His own bishop's rolls are the first of their kind and the oldest surviving for any part of Europe. Hugh was a good pastoral bishop, supporting priests and their congregations at a local level. Despite being absent from England for his first five years as bishop, he spent the next 21 years as a reforming bishop, active in his diocese. He died in 1235.

Although Hugh of Wells spent much of his time in other parts of the huge diocese, he had a strong influence on Lincoln. The building of a great Gothic cathedral begun by Hugh of Avalon was steadily continuing, despite the Interdict. Hugh of Wells petitioned the Pope for the canonisation of Hugh of Avalon, who was declared a saint in 1220, 20 years after his death. Stories of miracles at the tomb of St Hugh made Lincoln Cathedral a busy centre for pilgrimage, and later led to further extension of the building.

Reconstruction view of Lincoln Cathedral showing building work going on during the 13th century.

A HALL FIT FOR A KING

A remarkable hall in the Bishop's Palace on the south side of Lincoln Cathedral was begun by Bishop Hugh of Avalon and finished by Bishop Hugh of Wells. Perhaps in anticipation of a royal visit, the Close Rolls record that in 1223 Henry III allowed stone to be dug from the Lincoln city ditch near the palace for work to the hall and kitchen. In the next year, the king promised 40 trees from his forest of Sherwood for beams and joists for the hall. The resulting building was comparable with the great hall begun in the 1220s at the royal castle of Winchester. Its length is about 90 feet (around 27 metres). Its side aisles with large windows were separated from the central aisle by piers of Purbeck marble. The ruins of this impressive hall can still be seen in the Medieval Bishop's Palace, an English Heritage site which is open to the public.

The ruins of the Lincoln Medieval Bishop's Palace. On the left are the large double window openings of the west hall begun by St Hugh and completed by Bishop Hugh of Wells.

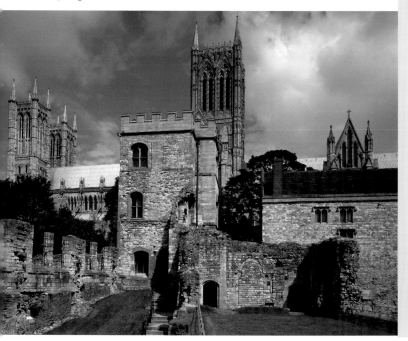

AN END TO CONFLICT

This charter of King John, dated 28 June 1213, is addressed to Bishop Hugh II of Lincoln. It notifies him that the king has granted peace and security to the English Church, according to the form laid down by Pope Innocent III. This brought to an end the five-year conflict between King and Pope (the Interdict) during which churches throughout England were closed and the people deprived of spiritual ministry.

King John's charter sent to Bishop Hugh of Wells to tell him that the papal Interdict had been lifted.

agna Carta's limitation of the king's powers was radical, unprecedented and revolutionary. Its overall message was that the law was supreme and the king himself was not above the law. But it also sought to establish, via a committee of 25 barons, an authority superior to the king. As such it was far ahead of its time. No medieval king could have accepted, without reservations, such a limitation on his authority.

It is clear that John had no intention of abiding by the Charter. Within weeks he was writing to the Pope, asking to be released from an oath exacted from him by force. John had declared 'by the honour of God' in the opening words of Magna Carta

Left: The heraldic shield of William de Mowbray, Lord of Axholme, who was one of the Committee of Twenty-Five Barons set up at Runnymede to hold the king to his word.
Below: Prince Louis of France arrives in a ship to invade England (MS 16, Parker Library).

to abide by its terms. Only the Pope could release him from this sacred oath. Innocent III's reply, exonerating the king and condemning those responsible for Magna Carta, reached England in September. Even before then John had broken the terms of the agreement by holding on to castles he should have surrendered, by hiring foreign mercenaries and generally preparing for armed resistance.

The east side of Lincoln Castle, with the 19th-century Observatory Tower on the left and the medieval east gate on the right.

PRINCE LOUIS INVADES ENGLAND

Fighting began in mid-September. Despite the setbacks he had received, John's position was a strong one and the rebels took the decision at the end of 1215 to invite Prince Louis, eldest son of the King of France, to invade England, depose John and take the throne. Louis landed in May 1216. Joining the rebels, he established control over London and much of eastern England. The only two strongholds left to John in this region were Dover and Lincoln castles, and both were closely besieged.

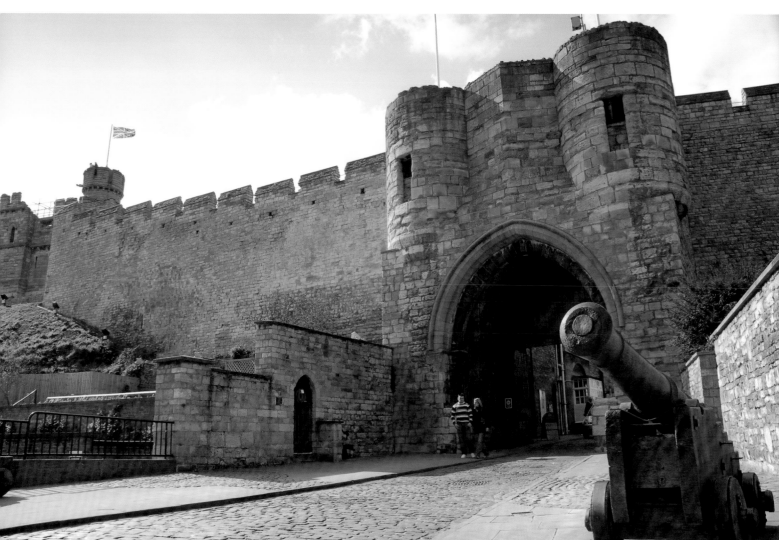

Louis of France sent troops to Lincoln under the command of the local rebels, Gilbert de Gant and Robert of Ropsley. In August they took the city of Lincoln, but not the castle. By this time Gerard de Canville was dead, and his wife Nicola de la Haye was constable of the castle. She resisted the attempt by Louis's troops to take the castle by buying them off.

A story (recorded many years afterwards) describes John meeting Nicola at Lincoln Castle. This encounter reveals another side to the king's character than that of the ruthless tyrant usually portrayed. Lady Nicola went out of the eastern gate carrying the keys of the castle in her hand. She met the king and offered the keys to him as her lord, saying she was a woman of great age and was unable to bear the burden of office any longer. John said, 'My beloved Nicola, I will that you keep the castle as hitherto until I shall order otherwise.' She retained the office of constable for another decade, not resigning until 1226.

JOHN LOSES HIS TREASURE – AND HIS LIFE

John was in Lincoln in late September 1216. In early October he led his troops to Grimsby, then south to Louth and Boston, ravaging the Lincolnshire countryside as he went. Taking ship at Spalding he sailed across the Wash to the port of Lynn (now King's Lynn) in Norfolk. According to contemporary accounts, he fell ill there and decided to return. It was while travelling back to Lincolnshire that he lost his treasure. He sent his baggage train, including the crown jewels, along a causeway usable only at low tide. Owing to a misreading of the tides, the baggage train was

Left: This fragment of the seal of Nicola de la Haye shows her elaborate dress. A bird of prey rests on her hand.
Below: At the east gate where Nicola de la Haye met King John, modern judges process from the Crown Court in Lincoln Castle to a service in Lincoln Cathedral at the beginning of a new session.

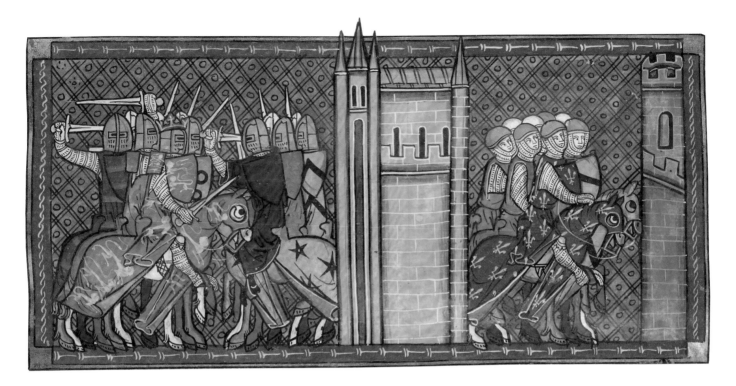

swamped by high tide, which swept away horses, wagons, drivers and riches. Modern historians are generally sceptical about this account, and most agree that John lost only a small part of his treasure. Making his way north via Swineshead, he stayed at the castles of Sleaford and Newark, both residences of the bishop of Lincoln. He died of dysentery at Newark Castle on the night of 18 October 1216.

John's death, and the accession of his nine-year-old son as Henry III, transformed the situation. Much of the baronial opposition had been to John personally and to his arbitrary style of government. The guardians of the young king, William Marshal (the Earl of Pembroke) and the Pope's legate in England, Guala Bicchieri, took the unexpected but strategically astute move of re-issuing Magna Carta, to rally support. This had the effect of bringing some of the barons back to the king's side. The culmination of the civil war was reached at a battle known as the Second Battle of Lincoln, in May 1217, when the siege of the castle was raised and many of the rebels were captured.

Above: King John in battle with Prince Louis of France, from the 14th-century *Chroniques de France ou de St Denis* (Royal MS 16 G VI, British Library).
Below: The Wash is the estuary where four rivers from Lincolnshire and Norfolk flow into the North Sea.

Now that John was dead, Gilbert de Gant, created earl of Lincoln by Prince Louis, returned to Lincoln to resume the siege of the castle, with Louis following. Despite their efforts to take the castle, Nicola continued her resistance and would not surrender. Louis returned to London and sent Hugh, the castellan of Arras, to set up quarters in Lincoln. Hugh convinced the rebellious barons that the castle was about to fall, and as a result the whole army of the rebel barons joined the French troops, quartered in and around Lincoln.

The king's guardians took charge. William Marshal mustered troops at Newark, while the

The 12th-century silver seal matrix was used to impress wax with the seal of the Dean and Chapter of Lincoln on official documents. It survived the ransacking of the cathedral's treasure during the Battle of Lincoln Fair.

papal legate Guala Bicchieri used spiritual inducements. He excommunicated Louis and all his accomplices, especially those besieging Lincoln Castle, together with the city of Lincoln, who supported the rebel barons, and the French army. He granted plenary absolution (full forgiveness of sin and remission of its punishment in Purgatory), to all who confessed their sins and supported the king's army. In effect the royalist cause was now preached as a crusade, with the royalist army wearing white crosses like crusaders.

Left: According to accounts of the Battle of Lincoln Fair, royalist troops entered the castle from the countryside through the west gate.
Below: Mounting a two-pronged attack, the royalist army entered Lincoln from the north, through the Roman gate called Newport Arch.

LINCOLN UNDER VIOLENT ASSAULT

The Bishop of Winchester, Peter des Roches, organised the attack. He knew the land, having been precentor at the cathedral. The Count of Perche, who commanded the French troops, mistakenly assessed the royalist forces gathering to the west of Lincoln as superior to his own. Instead of attacking he decided to keep his forces within the city walls. Accounts of the battle differ. According to the chronicler Roger of Wendover, prior of Belvoir at the time, the royalist Falkes de Breauté and his crossbowmen entered the west gate of the castle from the open countryside, climbed the castle walls and rained arrows down on the besiegers within the city. Mounting a two-pronged attack, the rest of the royalist army entered Lincoln through Newport Arch, the Roman north gate of the city. They advanced south along Bailgate while Falkes made a sally from the castle. Falkes was taken prisoner, but then rescued. When the Count of Perche was killed, the French troops fled. Exulting in their victory, the royalist troops seized the valuables of the defeated troops and sacked the city. According to Roger of Wendover they 'despoiled the whole city, even to the utmost farthing'. The papal legate had urged the troops to treat the canons of the cathedral as excommunicates for not supporting the king. They pillaged the cathedral and the city's churches, seizing gold and silver, jewels and rich vestments. A huge amount of the cathedral's silver was stolen from the precentor, Geoffrey of Deeping. Women and children took to boats on the River Witham, but the boats became overloaded and capsized, and their occupants were killed.

A DECISIVE VICTORY

Although the textbook name for this battle is the Second Battle of Lincoln, it is better known by what it was called at the time. 'The Fair' or 'the Battle of Lincoln Fair' are ironic names to describe the upheaval, bloodshed and flight of the citizens of Lincoln, and the rich pickings gained by the victors.

This was the decisive battle that signalled the end of the civil war after the death of King John. Three months later, in a naval engagement off the coast of Kent, French reinforcements were lost at sea, and Prince Louis gave up his claim to the English throne.

This vivid rendition of the battle shows royalist archers on the battlements of the castle, loosing arrows on the English rebels and French troops (MS 16, Parker Library).

R emarkably for such a famous document, the 1215 Magna Carta was in force for less than nine weeks. Once it was rejected by the king and the Pope its importance could have faded away. Its usefulness, however, lay in placating the rebellious barons who later gave their support to Prince Louis. It was usual for English kings to issue coronation charters, in which they swore to uphold the laws of the Anglo-Saxon past, showing their intention to honour ancient rights and liberties. John's son, the nine-year-old King Henry III, was crowned in Gloucester. A fortnight later, on 12 November 1216, Magna Carta was re-issued with revisions as just such a coronation charter supplementing the king's coronation oath.

In the autumn of the following year, 1217, the king re-issued Magna Carta with further revisions. This marked the conclusion of a peace treaty with Prince Louis, who returned to France. It was sealed by the boy king's chief minister, William Marshal, and the papal legate representing the Pope, Guala Bicchieri. Pope Innocent III had died and the new Pope, Honorius III, gave Magna Carta papal support. It would be difficult from now on to revoke.

A CHARTER FOR THE FOREST

A major difference in the 1217 reissue was that the clauses in Magna Carta dealing with the administration of the royal forests were now given more detail in a separate document, the Forest Charter. Only two originals of the 1217 Forest Charter survive: one belongs to Lincoln Cathedral, and the other is in the archives of Durham Cathedral. From this

Left: Engraving of the seal of Henry III (John Speed, *The History of Great Britaine*, London, 1614).

Below: The Charter of the Forest set out to return Forest Law to the way it was during the reign of King Henry II.

date, whenever the Great Charter was re-issued, the Little Charter, known as the Charter of the Forest, was issued with it. When it was perceived that the king was exceeding his powers, there were public calls to uphold 'the Charters'.

Left: William Marshal's tomb effigy in the Temple Church, London.
Right: Pope Honorius III and his cardinals listen to St Francis preaching, from a fresco by Giotto in the upper church of the Basilica of St Francis, Assisi, Italy.

THE ROYAL FORESTS

Under the Norman and Plantagenet kings, huge tracts of land that fell within the boundaries of the royal forests covering almost a third of England were subject to 'forest law' and not to common law. These areas were for the king's hunting and included not just woodland, but marsh, heath, scrubland, even villages in or near woodland. In the early 13th century, all land was held by the king, but entrusted to knights, abbots and priors of religious houses to farm and administer, in exchange for service to the king. The expansion of the royal forests was seen as an infringement on the rights of the king's vassals who looked after this land.

Anyone living in a royal forest under King John faced severe punishments for hunting with dogs, felling trees, grazing animals and generally trying to make a living there. They could incur sentences of maiming or even the death penalty if they were found guilty of trespassing against the game (the 'venison') or the natural habitat of the game (the 'vert'). Richard FitzNeal, one of John's officials, stated, 'The Forest has its own laws, based ... not on the common law of the realm, but on the arbitrary decision of the ruler.'

THE FOREST CHARTER, 1217

Like the 1215 Magna Carta, the Forest Charter is made of sheepskin parchment, and the writing is in ink made of a mixture of water and gall. Gall is a black substance found in oak apples, created when female gall wasps lay eggs in leaf buds. Originally the Charter had two seals attached to it, only one of which survives. The missing seal is that of the Earl Marshal, the young king's guardian, described in the Charter as 'ruler of us and our minister', and the surviving green beeswax seal is that of Guala Bicchieri, the papal legate.

A huntsman aiming an arrow at two beavers, from an English Bestiary of the early 13th century (Fitzwilliam Museum, Cambridge).

There are 17 chapters or clauses, which pledge to turn the clock back to the time of Henry II, the young king's grandfather. In general, land taken ('afforested') after the reign of Henry II is to be freed from forest law, or 'deforested' (clauses 1, 3, 4, 5). The treatment of dogs is to be more lenient. Expediating or lawing of dogs was the cutting off of the front claws to make the dogs of no use for hunting. The Charter indicates that at that time forest officials might go further than clipping only the claws, mutilating the ball of the dog's foot as well. Clause 6 makes it clear that the ball of the dog's foot should not be maimed. The forest officials were not to levy taxes in the form of grain or animals (clause 7). The forest court ('swanimote') was to take place regularly three times a year in order to hear offences against 'vert' and 'venison,' and to receive 'pannage-dues' (payment for pasturing swine in the forest).

No one was to lose life or limb if convicted of taking venison, but fined or imprisoned instead (clause 10). In areas outside the woods, scrub and moorland, every freeman was allowed to farm, and to have a mill, a clay pit and a pond (clause 12). He was also allowed to hunt for birds and to keep bees (clause 13).

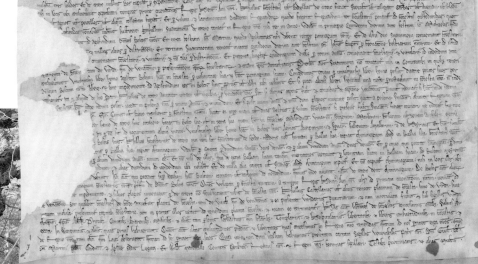

Above: Lincoln Cathedral's Forest Charter of 1217 is displayed with the 1215 Magna Carta in Lincoln Castle.
Left: The 800-year-old Major Oak in Sherwood Forest has associations with Robin Hood. This royal forest comprised 100,000 acres of woodland and heath, stretching over 30 miles from Nottingham to Worksop.

Henry III confirmed Magna Carta in its definitive version in 1225. During the course of his long reign until his death in 1272, he felt compelled more than ten times to uphold the 'Charters of Liberties,' usually by means of letter rather than by issuing the Charters again.

Robert Grosseteste, Bishop of Lincoln, recorded the views of the English bishops about the king's interference with the government of the Church, in contravention of the first clause of Magna Carta. These views formed the basis of the complaints made by the bishops at the Parliament at Oxford in 1258. At this Parliament, the barons who followed Simon de Montfort set out their ideas for reform. The idea of a royal 'Parliament' had already emerged by the 1230s. The king could gather his barons whenever he wished, wherever he happened to be. But if the barons wanted to meet the king, they could not call a Parliament themselves. In the Provisions of Oxford the barons called for regular parliaments to be held every three years, stating that in addition to the barons there should be non-noble representatives from the counties. Henry rejected their ideas.

Civil war broke out again. The barons defeated the king at the Battle of Lewes in May 1264. In January 1265 de Montfort called his own Parliament to discuss the peace terms. This gathering included for the first time representatives from each county, and from the cities and towns – a model for Parliament as it is known today. De Montfort was killed in battle only a few months later. The king now re-issued the Charters as part of his peace negotiations.

PARLIAMENT'S TAXATION DEMANDS

Henry's son Edward I faced a constitutional crisis over the manner in which he raised money to pay for wars, both in the island of Britain and abroad. In 1297, in addition to

Above: Magna Carta was written out for easy reference in statute books. A portrait of King Edward I appears within the first letter of his name (*Vetera Statuta*, Harley MS 858, British Library). *Left:* The scholar Robert Grosseteste (Bishop of Lincoln 1235–53) raised awareness that Henry III had contravened the 'Charter of Liberties'.

Left: This statue of Simon de Montfort, Earl of Leicester, is at the base of the 1868 Haymarket clock tower in the centre of Leicester.
Right: King Edward I and Queen Eleanor attended the dedication of the Angel Choir in Lincoln Cathedral in 1280. Ten years later, Eleanor died on pilgrimage to Lincoln. Her viscera were interred in the Angel Choir.

increased custom duties already imposed, the king ordered a new tax on moveable wealth, and compulsory sale of merchants' wool to the Crown for re-sale at a profit, in order to finance a war in Flanders. He also ordered the barons to fight alongside him in Flanders, a place where their ancestors had never before fought for the king. He levied a tax on the English clergy's goods, without consulting the Church, on the grounds that this taxation was necessary for the defence of the realm. The king's opponents met him in July in Stratford, near London, with a list of complaints. The *Monstraunces* (or Remonstrances) stated that:

> *all the community of the land … feel themselves greatly aggrieved in that they used to be treated according to the clauses of the Great Charter, whose clauses are all neglected to the great loss of the people.*

In October, while the king was overseas, his son and acting regent, Edward of Caernarvon, called a Parliament. Six articles were drawn up, called the Confirmation of the Charters. Articles 5 and 6 ensured that the contested taxes would not constitute a precedent, and that the king would not levy new taxes or export duties without 'the common assent of all the realm and for the common profit of the same realm'. On his return Edward I agreed to confirm Magna Carta, and sent letters to all the counties, accompanied by Magna Carta and the Forest Charter, which were to be read publicly throughout the land.

This 1225 version of Magna Carta, confirmed by Edward I in 1297, thereafter became the standard version of the text. Copies of it were made for lawyers, including pocket-sized versions for ease of reference, for use by travelling judges. This same version was used in the first printed editions in the 16th and 17th centuries. Four originals of the 1297 Magna Carta survive, one of which is today in the National Archives in Washington, D.C.

In 1301 Edward I held a Parliament at Lincoln, which is thought to have taken place partly in the Chapter House of the cathedral. The king was pressed to agree to eliminate those statutes which were against Magna Carta. Edward was angered by this bill, but in the end he agreed that any statutes that were contrary to the Charters were to be corrected 'by the common counsel of our realm … or even annulled'.

Edward III's Parliaments went a step further by reinterpreting Magna Carta, most notably passing a statute in 1354 extending the rights to 'due process of law' in clause 39. Instead of limiting this right to free men, the provision now extended to any man 'of whatever estate or condition he may be'.

MAGNA CARTA LAID ASIDE

Magna Carta and the Charter of the Forest were re-confirmed more than 30 times in the 14th century and eight times in the 15th century. Even so, during the 16th century, the Charters seem to have been forgotten by the general public.

A rise in antiquarian interest, and the printing press, gradually raised awareness of Magna Carta in this period. In 1533 John Leland was given access by Henry VIII to the libraries of cathedrals and religious houses to record their buildings, holdings and history. He listed books and manuscripts in the libraries of religious houses which were soon to be dissolved. He travelled in the British Isles, making notes on topography and history. This study remained in manuscript until it was published in the 18th century as *The Itinerary of John Leland in or about the years 1535–1543*. In 1508 Richard Pynson, Henry VIII's printer, produced the first printed version of the 1297 issue of Magna Carta. The first printed English translation of Magna Carta, by the politician, lawyer

Edward I's Parliament of January 1301 was held in Lincoln, possibly in the cathedral's Chapter House.

and poet George Ferrers, appeared in 1534. Matthew Parker was Master of Corpus Christi College, Cambridge and later Archbishop of Canterbury. He searched various private libraries and gathered together manuscript versions and fragments of the chronicle of Matthew Paris, a 13th-century monk of St Albans. In 1571 Parker arranged to have the work printed under the title of *Historia Maior*. It spans the period from William the Conqueror to Henry III. What Paris recorded as the 1215 text of Magna Carta was actually taken from the 1217 and 1225 versions. In 1577 and 1587 Richard Tottel, who had the royal patent to print law books, produced more accurate Latin versions of the 1225 Magna Carta. Ralph Holinshed's *Chronicle* of 1577, which includes an account of King John at Runnymede, was used as a source for William Shakespeare's history plays. Rebellion against a crowned and anointed king is a theme which appears in both Holinshed and Shakespeare. It was becoming easier to look to the past to inform the present.

Historia Maior, a chronicle of English history from 1066, was written by Matthew Paris (*c*.1200–59). It was rediscovered by Matthew Parker, who published this first printed edition in 1571.

Left: During the reign of Henry VIII (1509–47) Magna Carta was regarded largely as a document of antiquarian interest.
Below: Matthew Parker (1504–75) was Dean of Lincoln before becoming Archbishop of Canterbury.

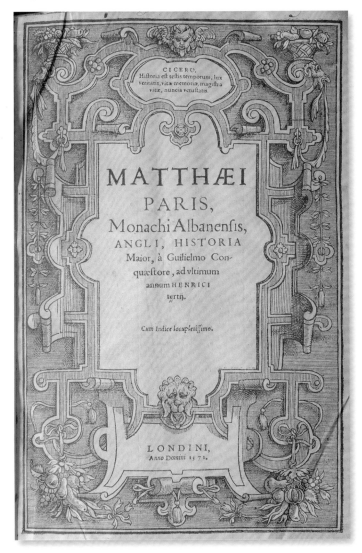

CICERO.
Historia est testis temporum, lux veritatis, vitæ memoriæ, magistra vitæ, nuncia vetustatis.

MATTHÆI
PARIS,
Monachi Albanensis,
ANGLI, HISTORIA
Maior, à Guilielmo Con-
quæstore, ad vltimum
annum HENRICI
tertij.

Cum Indice locupletissimo.

LONDINI,
Anno Domini 1571.

In the early 17th century, both James I and his son Charles I propounded a belief in the divine right of kings, which in theory placed them above the law. Lawyers such as Sir Edward Coke and John Selden interpreted Magna Carta to mean that although the king's authority might be God-given, his power was limited by Parliament, itself placed under the rule of law. The king must not tax his people without their consent, or imprison them without just cause. The lawyers of the 17th century invested Magna Carta with an almost mythical status, suggesting that it was one of the mainstays of an ancient constitution, itself, supposedly, far older than the power of kings. Yet they muddled the texts, often assuming that the text of the 1225 Magna Carta was the same as the one issued by King John in 1215. Coke assumed that Magna Carta was first issued as a charter of liberties for all, when it was originally intended to protect the rights of free men only. However vague all of this might be, Magna Carta was nonetheless viewed as a charter of ancient rights against the limitless power of the king. As such it was a useful tool against absolutism.

THE PETITION OF RIGHT

In 1627, in a case before the Court of King's Bench, five knights objected to the forced loans the king had demanded of them to raise money for war with France. The knights were imprisoned, but they insisted the Crown

Like his father James I, King Charles I thought that he was divinely appointed by God, and therefore could impose taxes without the consent of Parliament (Henry Holland, *Herwologia Anglia,* London, 1620).

show just cause. If there was no just cause they demanded release. Thomas Darnel, John Corbet, Walter Earl, John Heveningham and Edmund Hampden petitioned the King's Bench for a writ of habeas corpus. The attorney general replied that they were being held 'by the special command of his majesty'.

In 1628 Sir Edward Coke with John Selden drafted the Petition of Right for the House of Commons. The petition affirmed, among other things, that arbitrary imprisonment was illegal, as were forced loans and taxation without parliamentary consent. The petition cites Magna Carta as a precedent for these liberties. King Charles accepted the Petition of Right, but became less and less inclined to summon Parliament. Instead, he sought to rule via his ministers and by personal command.

UNFAIR TAXATION, WAR AND REGICIDE

Both James I and Charles I had long periods of 'personal rule'. James governed without summoning Parliament between 1614 and 1621; Charles did the same for an even longer period, between 1629 and 1640. Not wishing to call Parliament to approve new taxes, he resorted to alternative means. From 1634 Charles tried to make the entire kingdom pay a tax for coastal defence, which up until then only ports had paid. His lawyers upheld this extension of 'ship money'

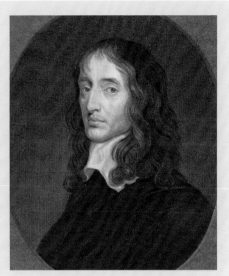
on the grounds that coastal defence was necessary for the safety of the nation. But it was a deeply unpopular tax.

Eventually Charles was obliged to summon Parliament to pay for fighting in Scotland, over the issue of whether or not the Scottish Church should have bishops. The Short Parliament lasted from April to May 1640. Charles summoned Parliament again later that year. The Long Parliament sat from November 1640 until it was dissolved by Oliver Cromwell in April 1653. This Parliament sought to limit the king's royal prerogative, even demanding control of the military. In January 1642 the king entered Parliament with 400 soldiers and attempted to arrest five members on a charge of treason, but failed. In August that year, Charles raised his standard in Nottingham Castle, marking the beginning of civil war between king and Parliament. The conflict resulted in his defeat. The same Long Parliament ordered the king's beheading, which took place in January 1649.

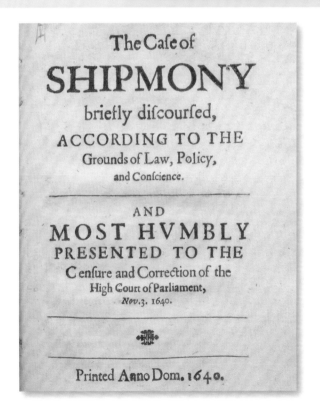

The Case of
SHIPMONY
briefly difcourfed,

ACCORDING TO THE
Grounds of Law, Policy,
and Confcience.

AND
MOST HVMBLY
PRESENTED TO THE
Cenfure and Correction of the
High Court of Parliament,
Nov.3. 1640.

Printed Anno Dom. 1640.

In *The Case of Shipmony*, the barrister Henry Parker took issue with Charles I for converting a tax on ports into a general tax, without consulting Parliament.

John Lilburne (1615–57) fought for Parliament in the Civil War. He criticised the powerful Long Parliament, which itself threatened to act no less arbitrarily than a tyrannical king. He was imprisoned several times for his views, and for printing pamphlets without license. As a leader of the movement called the Levellers, Lilburne believed in 'freeborn rights'. He maintained that all men and women are equal, and that the civil liberties in Magna Carta are for everyone. Accused of High Treason, he demanded a public trial by jury, insisting that he was entitled to this by Magna Carta, having studied Sir Edward Coke's *Institutes of the Lawes of England*. He was granted a jury trial in 1649 and was acquitted. While imprisoned in the Tower of London he wrote with William Walwyn, Thomas Prince and Richard Overton the third edition of *An Agreement of the Free People of England. Tendered as a Peace-Offering to this distressed Nation* (1647–49). They hoped the Agreement would be circulated and signed like a national petition, to form the basis for a written constitution for the Commonwealth. This work may have influenced the authors of the US Constitution and Bill of Rights.

CROMWELL REJECTS MAGNA CARTA

After the execution of Charles I, the Commonwealth lasted little more than a decade, from 1649 to 1660. There were no precedents for a republic. A government official, the poet John Milton, called for 'great actions, above the form of law

John Lilburne holds Coke's *Institutes*, in the frontispiece to the second edition of *The Tryal of Lieutenant Colonel John Lilburne*. He called Magna Carta 'the ground of my freedom. I build upon the Grand Charter of England'.

and custom'. The Lord Protector Oliver Cromwell disdained Magna Carta, referring to it as 'Magna Farta'. Having dissolved the brief Rump Parliament by force in 1653, Cromwell set up his own 'parliament of saints' consisting of 140 'godly' men, whose task it was to write a constitution. After five months this assembly disbanded. The army wanted Cromwell to become king, but he declined. Soon after his death in the autumn of 1658, the government collapsed.

THE 1689 BILL OF RIGHTS

At the Restoration of the Monarchy in 1660, Charles II was thanked by the Speaker of the House at his first Parliament 'for restoring to us our Magna Carta liberties'. This was a modernising Parliament, investing itself with more control of taxation. But there were concerns over the succession, as Charles's brother and heir, James, was a Catholic. Parliament considered excluding him from the throne. James II did take the throne, but became unpopular for favouring Catholics, replacing Anglicans with Catholics in posts such as Oxford University fellowships. In 1688 William of Orange, ruler of the Netherlands, invaded England. James II fled, and a Convention Parliament offered the Crown to William and his wife Mary, James's daughter. To secure a Protestant succession, Parliament named Mary's sister Anne to succeed her should William and Mary die childless.

Above: After Charles I's execution, a satirical cartoon was printed showing Oliver Cromwell cutting down the royal oak, along with the Bible, Magna Carta and British liberties.

Right: After the 'Glorious Revolution' of 1688–89, William and Mary were painted as joint Protestant monarchs by James Thornhill on the ceiling of Christopher Wren's Painted Hall, The Royal Naval College, Greenwich.

This Parliament drafted a Bill of Rights, enacted in December 1689, which laid down that the monarch was to govern 'according to the statutes in Parliament agreed on and the laws and customs of the same'. No longer could the king issue decrees with the force of law, nor could he dispense with the law, neither could he levy tax nor maintain a standing army without the consent of Parliament. Jury trials and writs of habeas corpus were guaranteed.

Magna Carta, the Petition of Right and the Bill of Rights are often said to form the basis for Britain's 'unwritten constitution'. With these three documents, Parliament became a branch of government superior to the monarchy, and the judiciary was safeguarded against interference by the Crown. This was the beginning of modern parliamentary democracy.

Right: The Restoration of the Monarchy, celebrated in *The entertainment of Charles II in his passage through the city of London to his coronation,* by John Ogilby (London, 1662).

DEVELOPING MAGNA CARTA PRINCIPLES

Most of the clauses in the 1215 Magna Carta were altered in the first ten years of its existence. During the 19th and 20th centuries, all but four of Magna Carta's original clauses were removed from the statute book. What remains are the clauses granting freedom to the Church (clause 1); guaranteeing the customs and liberties of the city of London (clause 13); and a promise that the king would not use his power to order arbitrary arrest, or to sell justice, and to guarantee judgement by one's equals (clauses 39 and 40).

In the clauses still in force, and one or two others, 17th-century lawyers found a basis for fundamental English rights and privileges, developing laws based on equality before the law, trial by jury, habeas corpus, freedom from arbitrary arrest, and parliamentary control of taxation.

THE JURIST

Sir Edward Coke (1552–1634) equated Magna Carta clauses 39 and 40 with the guarantee of 'due process of law'. Although the idea of trial by jury was not fully developed in the 13th century, he cited clause 39 as the basis for a modern jury trial. Coke's regard for the Great Charter is shown in his famous quote, 'Magna Charta is such a fellow, that he will have no sovereign.'

Sir Edward Coke contributed to the drafting of the first charter of the Virginia Company, granted by James I in 1606. This charter promised to allow the colonists all the liberties enjoyed by Englishmen. These liberties were also guaranteed in the charters of Massachusetts (1629), Maryland (1632), Connecticut (1662), Rhode Island and Carolina (both 1663), and Georgia (1732).

Sir Edward Coke.

William Penn.

Sir William Blackstone.

Edmund Burke.

William Pitt the Elder, First Earl of Chatham.

THE QUAKER

In 1687 William Penn (1644–1718), the English-born founder of Pennsylvania, published *The Excellent Priviledge of Liberty and Property Being the Birth-right of the Free-born Subjects of England*. It contains the first copy of Magna Carta printed on American soil. Penn echoed Coke in the belief that Magna Carta expressed fundamental and ancient rights for all. His democratic principles inspired the framers of the US Constitution.

THE LEGAL SCHOLAR

As a judge of the Court of Common Pleas, Sir William Blackstone (1723–80) became an authority on Common Law. His *Commentaries on the Laws of England* (1765–69) is a textbook for lawyers in England and North America, which is still studied today. The four volumes explain the law for the rights of persons, the rights of things (property law), private wrongs (torts), and public wrongs (criminal law).

The *Commentaries* helped to define Common Law. Published just before the American Revolution, this work was influential in the adoption of Common Law by the United States and other English-speaking countries. Blackstone was the first modern commentator properly to distinguish between the versions of Magna Carta issued in 1215 and 1225.

THE STATESMEN

Both Edmund Burke (1729–97) and William Pitt the Elder, First Earl of Chatham (1708–78) spoke in Parliament supporting the American colonists' protests against taxation without representation. Burke urged consent for the colonists to 'sit down … to the feast of Magna Charta'. Pitt asked, 'If the people of Britain are not to be taxed, but by Parliament … does it not directly follow, that the colonists cannot, according to Magna Charta and the bill of rights be taxed by Parliament, so long as they continue unrepresented?'

The principle that the king could not tax without consent is enshrined in Magna Carta. Having been assured that they would have the same rights as Englishmen, the American colonists objected to being taxed by Parliament when they did not elect members of Parliament. King George III justified taxing the colonists by the need to pay off the debt of the Seven Years' War against the French in North America, and to establish a standing army in the American colonies. Patriots such as Patrick Henry, Samuel Adams, John Hancock and James Otis voiced their protest. Otis is famous for his stirring cry, 'Taxation without representation is tyranny!'

The Stamp Act of 1765 required legal documents, newspapers and other printed materials in the colonies to be printed on paper from London which carried a revenue stamp. Already the colonists were required to import and export all merchandise in English ships, passing only through English ports. They were forbidden to build factories capable of competing with those in England. The colonial assemblies united in protest, forming the Stamp Act Congress. They petitioned Parliament and the king. Pressure also came from British merchants and manufacturers, whose trade with the colonies was threatened by the economic problems created by the act. The Stamp Act was repealed in 1766, but there were other unfair taxes. The situation came to a head with the Boston Tea Party of 16 December 1773. The Tea Act earlier that year had made it mandatory

John Locke, from a 1740 edition of his *Works*. 'The end of law is not to abolish or restrain, but to preserve and enlarge freedom.'

for colonists to buy tea from the British East India Company. In protest, a band of colonists tipped a shipment of tea into Boston harbour.

THE US DECLARATION OF INDEPENDENCE

War broke out in 1775, and although the colonists declared independence in the following year, the American Revolutionary War continued until 1783. A new nation was emerging and inevitably the colonists turned to England for inspiration. The philosopher John Locke (1632–1704) had helped to write the Fundamental Constitutions of Carolina of 1669. Ideas from Locke's *Two Treatises of Government* (1690) influenced the founders of the United States.

Based on his study of Natural Law, Locke observed in his *Two Treatises* that people are 'by nature, all free, equal and independent' and 'man being born … with a title to perfect freedom, and uncontrolled enjoyment of all the rights and privileges of the law of nature, equally with any other man, or number of men in the world, hath by nature a power not only to preserve his life, liberty and estate, against the injuries and attempts of other men; but to judge and punish the breaches of that law in others, as he is persuaded the offence deserves …'. Locke criticized the Divine Right of Kings, stating that '… all peaceful beginnings of government have been laid in the consent of the people'. Although he was moving away from invoking ancient rights in Magna Carta, the social contract principles he developed relied on a balance of power between government and the governed.

The Declaration of Independence, composed by Thomas Jefferson, was signed on 4 July 1776. Its opening words echo Locke: 'We hold these truths to be self-evident, that all men are created equal, that they are endowed by their Creator with certain unalienable Rights, that among these are Life, Liberty, and the Pursuit of Happiness. That to secure these rights, Governments are instituted among Men, deriving their just powers from the consent of the governed.'

In 1787 a Constitutional Convention was called in Philadelphia to agree the Constitution. The first ten amendments to the Constitution are called the Bill of Rights.

affix the STAMP.

'This is the Place to

This satirical comment on the deadly effect of the Stamp Act was printed in the bottom right-hand corner of *The Pennsylvania Journal and Weekly Advertiser* on 24 October 1765.

In the Fifth Amendment, the Grand Jury clause and the Due Process clause are directly derived from Magna Carta: 'No person shall be held to answer for a capital, or otherwise infamous crime, unless on a presentment or indictment of a grand jury, except in cases arising in the land or naval forces, or in the militia, when in actual service in time of war or public danger; nor shall any person be subject for the same offense to be twice put in jeopardy of life or limb; nor shall be compelled in any criminal case to be a witness against himself, nor be deprived of life, liberty, or property, without due process of law; nor shall private property be taken for public use, without just compensation.'

John Trumbull's painting of the signing of the Declaration of Independence on 4 July 1776 is in the US Capitol Building in Washington, D.C.

Lincoln's 1215 Charter easily could have been destroyed during the chaos of the English Civil War. Instead it lay undisturbed and unrecognised among the extensive Dean and Chapter archives until the early 19th century. In 1800 the government established a Record Commission to ensure the preservation of official archives. They chose the Lincoln Magna Carta as the exemplar for the transcription published in the first volume of their *Statutes of the Realm* in 1810. In 1848 eminent members of the Archaeological Institute visited Lincoln and recorded their inspection of the document. It was at that time framed and hanging on the wall in a room in Exchequer Gate opposite the cathedral, the office of the Chapter Clerk Robert Swan.

When the British government requested that Lincoln's Magna Carta be sent to the British Pavilion at the New York World's Fair in 1939, concerns were raised about its safety at a time when Hitler was advancing in Europe. Gratitude to the Americans must have played a part in the Dean and Chapter's decision to let the Charter go. The Americans had given very generously to Dean Fry's appeals on visits to the United States to raise funds for urgent repairs to Lincoln Cathedral carried out between 1922 and 1932. At the World's Fair, Magna Carta was exhibited in its own hall within the British Pavilion, where it was seen by many Americans who appreciated its significance for the founding of the United States.

THE US GOVERNMENT SAFEGUARDS MAGNA CARTA

When Great Britain declared war on Germany in September 1939, it became clear that it would not be safe for such a precious document to return by sea to England. The British

A postcard of the New York World's Fair, 1939–40.

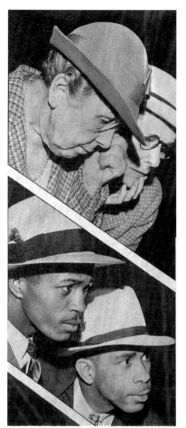

Left: Americans looking at Magna Carta in the Library of Congress. According to Dr Evans, the Librarian of Congress at the time, 15 million people saw Magna Carta in the USA.
Right: The Cathedral Clerk of Works, Robert S. Godfrey, opens Magna Carta's bullet-proof case on its return from the USA to Lincoln in January, 1946.

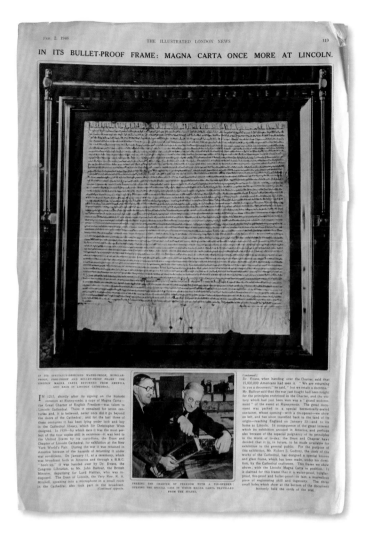

government requested that it should stay in the United States for the duration of the war, so it was sent to the Library of Congress in Washington, D.C. In 1941, in an extraordinary turn of events, the British government under Prime Minister Winston Churchill seriously considered making a gift of the Lincoln Magna Carta to the American people, as a means of encouraging their support at a crucial stage in the war. At no stage of the discussions does it seem to have occurred to Churchill that the Charter did not actually belong to the British government and was not theirs to give. Nor was any approach made to the Dean and Chapter of Lincoln to ascertain how they might view such a proposal. By the time the USA entered the war in December 1941, the matter had been dropped.

Concerned about national security, the US government started to make plans to safeguard their own most valued archives. It is a sign of the great importance placed on Magna Carta that they sent it to Fort Knox, Kentucky, one of only seven artefacts to be stored where the US gold reserves were guarded. The other items were the United States Articles of Confederation, the Declaration of Independence, the Constitution, Abraham Lincoln's Second Inaugural Address, Lincoln's Gettysburg Address, and three volumes of the Gutenberg Bible. Lincoln's Magna Carta returned to Lincoln Cathedral in 1946.

MAGNA CARTA AT HOME AND ON TOUR

Between 1976 and 1989 Dean Oliver Fiennes, whose ancestor Geoffrey Say was a baron at Runnymede, arranged for Magna Carta to travel extensively to numerous cities in the United States and Canada. In 1988 the Charter was exhibited at Expo '88 in Brisbane, Australia. To mark the 400th anniversary of the founding of the colony of Virginia (of which Lincolnshire's John Smith was first President), Magna Carta was displayed in 2007 in the *Contemporary Art Center of Virginia* in Virginia Beach, not far from where the first settlers landed. That July it was loaned to the US National Educational Association for an exhibition in the National Constitution Centre in Philadelphia. The Reagan Library in California hosted Magna Carta in July 2009, and later that year it was shown at Fraunces Tavern Museum in New York City by the Sons of the Revolution in the State of New York.

Leading up to the 800th anniversary, in 2014 Magna Carta went to The Museum of Fine Arts in Boston, then to The Clark Art Institute in Williamstown, Massachusetts. As the year closed it was at the Library of Congress, 75 years since its first sojourn there. On its return to England it went to London, where in February 2015 in the British Library it was joined by the three other 1215 exemplars in a 'unification' exhibition, for one day only, for 1215 ballot winners to see. A few days later, the four Charters were in the Robing Room of the House of Lords, accompanied in the Royal Gallery by iconic Parliamentary documents, such as the Petition of Right and the Bill of Rights. Members of both Houses of Parliament, invited Commonwealth representatives, and students savoured the occasion, a magnificent start to the anniversary celebrations.

On each of its travels, huge numbers of people of different ages and backgrounds have seen this ancient Charter.

Lincoln Cathedral's 1215 Magna Carta was first given a home in Lincoln Castle in 1992. In 2008 the Lincoln Cathedral 1217 Charter of the Forest was added. The David P.J. Ross Vault in Lincoln Castle was built in 1215 to display these two documents.

None of the barons and churchmen who met at Runnymede could have imagined the enormous importance of their short-lived peace treaty with King John. What is remembered is that Magna Carta established the precedent that the all-powerful king was made subject to the law. In addition, it is viewed as the origin of the principle of due process of law, a hallmark of democracy not only in Great Britain and its former colonies, but throughout the world.

Exhibition curator Nathan Dom discusses Lincoln Cathedral's Magna Carta with HRH The Princess Royal, Vice Admiral Sir Tim Laurence, and Sir Peter Westmacott, at the opening of the Library of Congress exhibition, *Magna Carta: Muse and Mentor*, in November 2014. Photo © 2014 John Harrington.